STATE BIRDS

★ ——————— ★

including the Commonwealth of Puerto Rico

Also by Elaine Landau

STATE BIRDS

INCLUDING THE COMMONWEALTH OF PUERTO RICO

BY ELAINE LANDAU

FRANKLIN WATTS

NEW YORK ★ CHICAGO ★ LONDON ★ TORONTO ★ SYDNEY

★ ━━━━━ ★

For the wonderful librarians
at state libraries throughout the country
who helped provide information for this book

Photographs copyright ©: Tom J. Ulrich: pp. 9, 10, 11, 14, 16, 20, 22, 24, 25, 29, 30, 35, 38, 39, 41, 42, 51, 54, 56, 57, 59; Florida Department of Commerce, Division of Tourism: pp. 12, 52; David Barron: p. 13; Raymond A. Mendez/ Animals Animals: p. 15; Ricardo E. Allen/ Delaware Tourism Office: p. 17; Visuals Unlimited: pp. 18 (Bill Beatty), 19, 32, 55, 60 (all John D. Cunningham), 23, 26, 36, 37, 53 (all S. Maslowski), 27, 40, 47 (all Tom J. Ulrich), 31 (Ted Whittenkraus), 34, 43, 50, 58 (all William J. Weber), 45 (Stephen J. Lang); Hawaii State Capitol, Governor's Office, Office of Information: p. 21; Louisiana Department of Wildlife & Fisheries: p. 28; Minnesota Department of Natural Resources: p. 33; Wyoming Game & Fish Department: p. 44; Oklahoma Department of Wildlife Conservation: p. 46; Pennsylvania Travel Marketing Bureau: p. 48; Rhode Island Department of Economic Development: p. 49.

Library of Congress Cataloging-in-Publication Data

Landau, Elaine.
State birds / by Elaine Landau.
p.   cm.
Includes bibliographical references and index.
Summary: Describes each state's official bird and how it was chosen.

ISBN 0-531-20058-2 (lib. bdg.) — ISBN 0-531-15629-X (pbk.)

1. State birds—United States—Juvenile literature.   [1. State birds.   2. Birds.   3. Emblems, State.]   I. Title.   II. Series.
QL699.L36   1992
598.2973—dc20   92-8949   CIP   AC

CONTENTS

★ ■■■■■■ ★

INTRODUCTION	7
ALABAMA Yellowhammer	9
ALASKA Willow Ptarmigan	10
ARIZONA Cactus Wren	11
ARKANSAS Mockingbird	12
CALIFORNIA California Valley Quail	13
COLORADO Lark Bunting	14
COMMONWEALTH OF PUERTO RICO	
Reinita Común	15
CONNECTICUT Robin	16
DELAWARE Blue Hen Chicken	17
DISTRICT OF COLUMBIA Wood	
Thrush	18
FLORIDA Mockingbird	19
GEORGIA Brown Thrasher	20
HAWAII Nene	21
IDAHO Mountain Bluebird	22
ILLINOIS Cardinal	23
INDIANA Cardinal	24
IOWA Eastern Goldfinch	25
KANSAS Western Meadowlark	26
KENTUCKY Cardinal	27
LOUISIANA Brown Pelican	28
MAINE Chickadee	29
MARYLAND Baltimore Oriole	30
MASSACHUSETTS Chickadee	31
MICHIGAN Robin	32
MINNESOTA Loon	33
MISSISSIPPI Mockingbird	34
MISSOURI Bluebird	35
MONTANA Western Meadowlark	36
NEBRASKA Western Meadowlark	37
NEVADA Mountain Bluebird	38

NEW HAMPSHIRE   Purple Finch   39
NEW JERSEY   Goldfinch   40
NEW MEXICO   Roadrunner   41
NEW YORK   Bluebird   42
NORTH CAROLINA   Cardinal   43
NORTH DAKOTA   Western Meadowlark   44
OHIO   Cardinal   45
OKLAHOMA   Scissor-Tailed Flycatcher   46
OREGON   Western Meadowlark   47
PENNSYLVANIA   Ruffed Grouse   48
RHODE ISLAND   Rhode Island Red
   Hen   49
SOUTH CAROLINA   Carolina Wren   50
SOUTH DAKOTA   Ring-Necked
   Pheasant   51
TENNESSEE   Mockingbird   52
TEXAS   Mockingbird   53
UTAH   Sea Gull   54
VERMONT   Hermit Thrush   55
VIRGINIA   Cardinal   56
WASHINGTON   Willow Goldfinch   57
WEST VIRGINIA   Cardinal   58
WISCONSIN   Robin   59
WYOMING   Western Meadowlark   60
FOR FURTHER READING   61
INDEX   62

INTRODUCTION

★ ▬▬▬▬▬▬▬▬ ★

Birds have always been a source of wonder and interest to people. They are important to both nature and humans in various ways. Birds have also long served as symbols of human characteristics or conditions. The owl standing for wisdom; the dove representing peace; and the eagle symbolizing military might are just a few examples.

Each state, as well as the District of Columbia and the Commonwealth of Puerto Rico, has adopted a state bird. A widespread movement among bird and garden clubs encouraged state legislators (lawmakers) to choose a bird to represent their state. The groups stressed that we cannot afford to take these feathered animals for granted. Since the first white settlers arrived on America's shores about eighty types of birds have become extinct. Some were killed off through hunting. Others died as forests and fields were turned into farms and towns.

The state birds were selected in a number of ways. In some states, schoolchildren were asked to vote for a state bird. Their ballots were cast as part of an educational program about different birds within their states. In other states, bird and garden clubs and conservation and educational groups held statewide contests in which residents were encouraged to vote for a state bird. In some cases, certain groups petitioned legislators to adopt a particular bird, while in others legislators on their own selected birds that were especially representative of the state. Some birds were chosen to call attention to the fact that they were endangered.

As you read this book about state birds, you will learn many interesting facts about the birds—and even about the states that chose them. Looking at birds is more fun if you know the stories behind the symbols.

Note: In this book the state birds are described state by state and the states are arranged in alphabetical order. Two names are given for every bird. The first is its common name, the one most people use to identify the bird. The second name, the one in brackets, is the name scientists use.

ALABAMA

Yellowhammer [*Colaptes auratus auratus*]

The yellowhammer is a North American woodpecker that usually grows to between 12 and 14 inches (30–36 cm) long. The bird has a brown face, a gray cap, and a brown back with black horizontal bars. The area beneath its wings and tail is yellow. Yellowhammers feed mostly on insects.

The yellowhammer was adopted as Alabama's state bird on September 6, 1927. It was chosen because the bird's colors seemed similar to the yellow-trimmed, gray uniforms worn by Confederate soldiers during the Civil War.

ALASKA

★ ▬▬▬ ★

Willow Ptarmigan [*Lagopus lagopus*]

The willow ptarmigan is a plump-bodied bird that lives in cold northern regions. During the warmer months, the male bird has reddish-brown and black feathers. In the winter, the feathers of both male and female turn as white as snow. The willow ptarmigan even has short white feathers on its feet for added warmth.

The white color allows the willow ptarmigan to blend in with the winter environment and thus helps protect the bird from its enemies. The willow ptarmigan sometimes hides in snowdrifts to escape danger.

Alaska's Department of Education and the Education Section of the Alaska Native Service ran a contest in which Alaskans were asked to vote for a bird to represent their state. The willow ptarmigan received more votes than any other bird. On February 4, 1955, Alaska's legislature officially adopted the bird.

▬▬▬

ARIZONA

Cactus Wren [*Heleodytes brunneicapillus*]

Wrens tend to be small active birds with slender bills and rounded wings. The cactus wren, Arizona's state bird, is the largest wren found in the United States. It grows to about 6½ inches (17 cm) long. The cactus wren has a brown back streaked with white and a black and white striped tail. It often nests in Arizona's cacti and thorny bushes.

The cactus wren is useful to humans because it destroys harmful insects. Both the Arizona Game Protective and the Conservation Committee of the state's Women's Club had suggested it be made Arizona's state bird. It was officially adopted by the state legislature on March 16, 1931.

ARKANSAS

★ ━━━━━━━ ★

Mockingbird [*Mimus polyglottos*]

The mockingbird is a slender bird that usually lives in the South, but has been spotted in many northern states as well as in Canada. The bird has an ash-gray coat, darker wings with white markings, and a whitish breast. It is about 9 inches (23 cm) long. Although the mockingbird has a pleasant song of its own, it is well known for copying other birds' songs. Mockingbirds feed on insects and wild fruits and berries.

The mockingbird became the state bird on March 5, 1929. It is also the state bird of *Florida*, *Mississippi*, *Tennessee*, and *Texas*. For more information, look under these states.

CALIFORNIA

★ ━━━━━━━━ ★

California Valley Quail [*Lophortyx californica*]

The California valley quail is a hardy, plump game bird that usually grows to about 10 inches (25 cm) long. Its coat, wings, breast, and tail vary in color from shades of gray to greenish brown. The male bird's throat is black with a white stripe beneath it. A black plume on the bird's head points downward.

During the day the California valley quail spends much of its time on the ground looking for food. It eats mainly grass, weeds, and acorns. At night it often perches in thick trees or shrubs, where it is hidden from predators.

At the close of the 1920s, the California Audubon Society conducted a poll to select a state bird. Of the twenty-two birds in the contest, the California valley quail received the most votes. It was officially adopted as California's state bird on June 12, 1931.

COLORADO

★ ■■■■■■■■■ ★

Lark Bunting [*Calamospiza melanocorys stejneger*]

The lark bunting is a seed-eating bird that sings in flight. These birds grow to a length of about 6 inches (15 cm). The female bird is gray streaked with brown, the male black and white. During the winter, however, the male's color becomes similar to the female's. The lark bunting is found in Colorado during the warm weather months. In the winter, flocks of these birds fly south to Mexico.

There had been some dispute among Colorado legislators in selecting a state bird. A number of officials wanted to adopt the meadowlark; others seemed set on the bluebird.

According to a story reported in a Denver newspaper, the lark bunting was eventually picked for purely practical reasons. It seems that the legislators had wanted a picture of the state bird to appear on all official stationery. But if a colorful bird were selected, the printing costs would skyrocket. (Printing in black and white costs much less than full-color printing.) To keep the price down, the legislators had to come up with a black and white state bird and the (male) lark bunting therefore seemed the perfect choice. The lark bunting was officially adopted as Colorado's state bird on April 29, 1931.

COMMONWEALTH OF PUERTO RICO

Reinita Común, or Bananaquit [*Coereba flaveola*]

The reinita común is a small West Indian songbird with a long curved beak. It is dark gray on top with a yellow underside. The bird also has a white stripe across its eye and a white wing spot. The reinita común primarily eats insects, although at times it feeds on flower nectar and ripe bananas that have split open.

The reinita común is often seen in gardens and open woodlands. It is found throughout the West Indies (except Cuba) and in southern Mexico, Argentina, Colombia, Venezuela, Brazil, and several other countries.

In 1980 Puerto Rico's legislature proposed making the reinita común the island's official bird. However, the bill was never voted on. Although the reinita común is generally still considered the national bird, some people believe that another bird called the pajero carintero should be awarded this honor. These people argue that while the reinita común inhabits the region, the pajero carintero is mainly found in Puerto Rico.

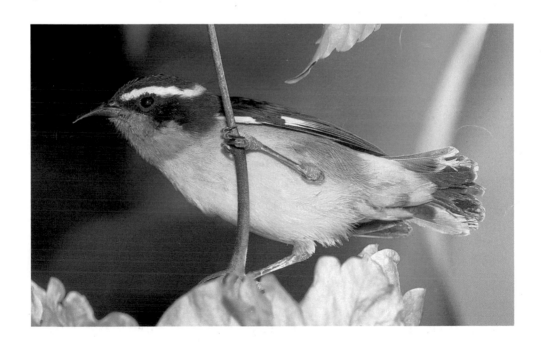

CONNECTICUT

★ ━━━━━━━━━ ★

Robin [*Turdus migratorius*]

The American robin is a popular North American bird known for its loud, cheery song. The top and sides of the robin's head are black, its wings and back are olive gray, and its breast is rusty red. The male bird, which usually grows to about 8½ to 10 inches (22–25 cm) long, tends to be a bit larger and more colorful than the female. Robins are eager eaters. They feed largely on earthworms and insects and on berries and various other small fruits.

The robin was adopted as Connecticut's state bird on March 27, 1943. It is also the state bird of *Michigan* and *Wisconsin*.

DELAWARE

★ ═══════════ ★

Blue Hen Chicken [*Gallus domesticus gallus*]

The Blue Hen chicken, a breed once used for cockfighting, was well known for its fierceness in the cockpit. During the American Revolution, when Delaware's fighting men went off to war, they often took along these slate-gray birds. During quiet times between battles, the men entertained themselves by pitting the male birds (cocks) against one another. Before long, word of the Blue Hen's bravery spread. And when Delaware soldiers fought valiantly against the British, they were compared to their own fighting birds.

The Blue Hen chicken has been the state bird since April 14, 1939. It is no longer used for cockfighting, which is now illegal in Delaware. But it has sometimes been used in political campaigns as a symbol of daring and courage.

DISTRICT OF COLUMBIA

Wood Thrush [*Hylocichla mustelina*]

The District of Columbia's official bird is the wood thrush, a songbird frequently found in the eastern United States. The wood thrush grows to about 7½ to 8½ inches (19–22 cm) long. The upper portion of its body is cinnamon brown, while its sides and underparts are white with black spots.

As its name suggests, the wood thrush often lives in wooded areas, where it feeds on insects and berries. Its song sounds very much like a flute.

The wood thrush was selected as the District of Columbia's official bird on January 31, 1967.

FLORIDA

★ ▬▬ ★

Mockingbird [*Mimus polyglottos*]

Florida officially made the mockingbird its state bird on April 23, 1907. Over 200,000 Florida schoolchildren—out of a possible 289,000—voted for it. Among the reasons given for its official adoption was that "the melody of its music has delighted the hearts of residents and visitors to Florida."

The mockingbird is described under *Arkansas*.

GEORGIA

Brown Thrasher [*Toxostoma rufum*]

The brown thrasher is an attractive bird with a rusty brown head and back. Its breast is white with brown streaks. Brown thrashers are fairly large birds; they may grow to 11½ inches (29 cm) in length. Brown thrashers do not have their own song; they mimic, or copy, the songs of other birds.

On April 6, 1935, the governor of Georgia declared the brown thrasher Georgia's state bird. Thirty-five years later, the Garden Clubs of Georgia requested that the bird be formally adopted by a vote of the state legislature. The legislature voted its agreement, so in 1970 the brown thrasher officially became Georgia's state bird.

HAWAII

★ ▬▬▬▬ ★

Nene (Hawaiian Goose) [*Branta sandvicensis*]

The nene, or Hawaiian goose, is an endangered wild bird with creamy-white ruffled neck feathers. The nene has longer legs and less foot webbing than most types of geese.

When the first Hawaiian settlers arrived, more than 25,000 nene inhabited the area. They lived on lava flows high on the slopes of volcanoes. There the birds enjoyed a diet of berries, weeds, and grasses, and were largely safe from predators.

The passage of time, however, brought the birds a much harder life. Increased hunting and new predators—such as dogs, cats, and the mongoose—brought to Hawaii by humans, threatened the birds' survival. In addition, a human invasion of the nene's breeding and nesting areas also caused the birds' numbers to lessen.

Alarmed by the bird's near disappearance, conservationists tried to save the nene. They bred the birds in a protected facility and then released them into the wild. Forty-five thousand acres (18,200 hectares) of protected area on the island were set aside to enable the nene to multiply and thrive. The nene has become a symbol for people concerned about the fate of all wild birds and animals facing extinction. On May 7, 1957, before Hawaii became a state, the territory's legislature adopted the nene as Hawaii's official bird, and it remains so today.

▬▬▬▬

IDAHO

★ ▬▬▬ ★

Mountain Bluebird [*Sialia currucoides*]

The mountain bluebird is a colorful songbird that often inhabits western mountain areas in North America. This sweet-sounding bird grows to about 6 to 7 inches (15–18 cm) in length. The male is sky blue with a white belly and a light-blue breast and throat. The female is brown with a bluish rump, tail, and wings. Mountain bluebirds feed on insects and wild fruits and berries.

The mountain bluebird often nests in tree hollows such as old woodpecker holes. After building its nest, this neat worker carries away any remaining debris from its home. In recent years, the number of mountain bluebirds has decreased. Human beings have played a role in their decline. Many acres of natural woodlands have been turned into farms. As a result, there are fewer trees for the birds to nest in as well as fewer wild fruits and berries for them to eat.

The mountain bluebird was made Idaho's state bird on February 28, 1931.

▬▬▬

ILLINOIS

★ ━━━━━ ★

Cardinal [*Richmondena cardinalis cardinalis*]

The popular cardinal is not only Illinois's state bird. It is also the state bird of *Indiana, Kentucky, North Carolina, Ohio, Virginia,* and *West Virginia.*

The cardinal is about 8 to 9 inches (20–23 cm) long with a pointed feather crest on its head. Although the male cardinal is primarily bright red, its back is shaded with gray. The female has a bright-red bill, and a yellowish-gray body with a dull-red tail, crest, and wings.

Cardinals eat insects as well as seeds from various weeds and fruits. This bird's song is so lovely that at one time cardinals were captured and sold as pets. The cardinal's feathers were also sometimes used to decorate hats, handbags, belts, and other items. Laws have since been passed to protect these attractive birds.

Illinois schoolchildren voted to select the cardinal as the state bird. The students were given ballots listing five popular birds and asked to vote for one. The cardinal proved to be the young people's favorite, while the bluebird came in second. The cardinal was officially made Illinois's state bird on June 4, 1929.

━━━━━

INDIANA

Cardinal [*Richmondena cardinalis cardinalis*]

In Indiana, the Audubon Society campaigned for the cardinal to become the state bird when it learned that Indiana was one of four states that had not already selected a state bird. On March 9, 1933, the cardinal was officially chosen to represent Indiana. The cardinal is described under *Illinois*.

IOWA

Eastern Goldfinch [*Spinus tristis tristis*]

The goldfinch is a songbird that grows to about 5 inches (13 cm) long. In the summer, the male is bright yellow with a black patch on its head, black wings, and a black tail. The female has a dull olive-yellow body and a black tail. In the winter, the male's coloring is very much like the female's.

Goldfinches are social birds. They are frequently seen gathering in small groups on tree branches. These birds are sometimes called wild canaries.

The goldfinch was adopted as Iowa's state bird on March 22, 1933. While many of Iowa's goldfinches fly as far south as Mexico for the winter, some now remain in the state throughout the year. Iowa residents have provided well-stocked bird feeders to be sure their state bird has enough to eat during the cold winter months.

The goldfinch is also the state bird of *New Jersey* and *Washington*.

KANSAS

Western Meadowlark [*Sturnella neglecta*]

The western meadowlark is a North American bird that grows to about 9 inches (23 cm) in length. The bird's back, wings, and tail are brown streaked with black. Its throat and underparts are bright yellow, with a large black V that marks the bird's breast.

The western meadowlark is known for its loud, gurgling, flutelike song. It also has an unusual flight pattern—a number of rapid wing beats followed by a brief span of smooth flying. These birds primarily inhabit meadows, plains, and prairies. They are helpful to humans because they eat harmful insects and large amounts of weed seeds.

Kansas schoolchildren voted to select the western meadowlark as the state bird. The state legislature made it official on June 30, 1937.

The western meadowlark is also the state bird of *Montana*, *Nebraska*, *North Dakota*, *Oregon*, and *Wyoming*.

KENTUCKY

Cardinal [*Richmondena cardinalis cardinalis*]

The cardinal was adopted as Kentucky's state bird on February 17, 1926. The bird has served as an important symbol for the state in sports, business, and education. The cardinal's image has been used by the University of Louisville's athletic teams as well as by Louisville's minor-league baseball team. Numerous Kentucky elementary schools bear the cardinal's name. A wide range of businesses named after this bird also appear in Kentucky telephone directories.

The cardinal is described under *Illinois*.

Female Cardinal

LOUISIANA

★ ━━━━━━━━━ ★

Brown Pelican [*Pelecanus occidentalis*]

The brown pelican, which grows to a length of about 4 feet (1.2 m), lives near the ocean. Although it looks clumsy on land, the bird is actually an excellent flyer. It has a large bill and throat pouch, which it uses to catch and hold fish.

Over fifty years ago, brown pelicans were quite common in Louisiana. Thousands of these birds nested in large colonies along Louisiana's gulf shore and inland bays. However, in the early 1960s, pesticides and environmental changes caused the brown pelican to nearly disappear. Louisiana's Department of Wildlife and Fisheries has taken steps to return these birds to the state. They've brought in young brown pelicans from other regions to protected wildlife areas along Louisiana's coasts.

On July 27, 1966, Louisiana, which had often been called the Pelican State, adopted the brown pelican as its state bird. The bird appears on both the state seal and state flag.

MAINE

Chickadee [*Parus atricapillus*]

Chickadees are small birds that inhabit much of North America's woodlands and usually grow to a length of 4½ to 5½ inches (11–14 cm). The black-capped chickadee has a black head and throat and a gray back. The bird's underside is an off-white color, and its tail is black with white outer feathers.

Chickadees nest in tree holes. They may frequently be seen hanging upside down from a branch to more easily catch their prey. The chickadee is named for its call, which sounds like chick-a-dee-dee-dee.

Maine adopted the chickadee as its state bird on April 16, 1927. It is also *Massachusetts*'s state bird.

MARYLAND

★ ▬▬▬▬▬ ★

Baltimore Oriole [*Icterus galbula*]

The Baltimore oriole, sometimes also called a firebird or golden robin, is a pleasant-sounding songbird. The male grows to a length of 7 to 8 inches (18–20 cm), while the female tends to be smaller. The male is also more brightly colored, with a black head and back and an orange breast. The female's back is brown, and her breast is yellow or rust-colored.

The Baltimore oriole was first noted in Maryland during colonial times. It was named after Lord Baltimore, the Maryland colony's governor. The male bird's orange and black feathers are the colors of Lord Baltimore's coat of arms. The Baltimore oriole was adopted as Maryland's state bird on June 1, 1947.

▬▬▬▬▬

MASSACHUSETTS

★ ———— ★

Chickadee [*Parus atricapillus*]

Both the Massachusetts Audubon Society and the Massachusetts Forest and Park Association wanted the chickadee as the official bird for their state. With the support of these groups, it was adopted by the state legislature on March 21, 1941.

The chickadee is described under *Maine*.

MICHIGAN

Robin [*Turdus migratorius*]

In Michigan, the Audubon Society held an election to determine the best-liked bird in the state. Of the nearly 200,000 ballots cast, the robin won the majority of votes. The Michigan legislature officially adopted this bird as its state bird on May 21, 1931.

The robin is described under *Connecticut*.

MINNESOTA

★ ══════════ ★

Loon [*Gavia immer*]

The loon is a water bird between 28 and 36 inches (71–91 cm) long. Its shiny green and black head and neck make it look like an oversized duck. The loon's back is black and its wings are speckled with white. It has large webbed feet and a pointed bill that is useful in catching fish. The loon's excellent diving ability also helps it to seize its prey. Loons are known for their eerie laughlike call that can sometimes be heard across bodies of water after nightfall.

The loon was officially adopted as Minnesota's state bird on March 13, 1961.

MISSISSIPPI

★ ▬▬▬▬▬▬ ★

Mockingbird [*Mimus polyglottos*]

The Mississippi Federation of Women's Clubs conducted a campaign to select a state bird. The campaign showed the mockingbird, commonly found throughout Mississippi, to be the favorite. It was officially adopted on February 23, 1944.

The mockingbird is described under *Arkansas*.

MISSOURI

★ ━━━━━━━ ★

Bluebird [*Sialia sialis*]

The bluebird is a colorful North American songbird that grows to about 7 inches (18 cm) in length. It is called a bluebird because its head, back, tail, and wings are bright blue. The bird's breast and throat are rusty brown, while its underparts are white. The female's coloring tends to be somewhat paler than the male's.

Bluebirds largely feed on insects and berries. These birds are often a welcome sight, since they destroy harmful insects yet don't ruin farm crops. The bluebird is frequently regarded as a symbol of happiness. It was adopted as Missouri's state bird on March 30, 1927.

The bluebird is also *New York*'s state bird.

MONTANA

★ ▬▬▬▬▬ ★

Western Meadowlark [*Sturnella neglecta*]

The western meadowlark was first spotted in Montana by Meriwether Lewis of the Lewis and Clark expedition to the Pacific Northwest. On June 22, 1805, the explorer wrote a detailed description of the bird in his journal. Through the years, the western meadowlark has been loved by Montana residents. When, in 1930, Montana schoolchildren cast their ballots to choose a state bird, it received the most votes. The Montana legislature officially made it the state bird on January 4, 1931.

The western meadowlark is described under *Kansas*.

NEBRASKA

Western Meadowlark [*Sturnella neglecta*]

In 1928 the Nebraska Federation of Women's Clubs voted to select a state bird. The western meadowlark won the contest. (The robin came in second.) When Nebraska schoolchildren were asked to pick their favorite bird, they chose the western meadowlark too. It was officially adopted as the state bird on March 22, 1929.

The western meadowlark is described under *Kansas*.

NEVADA

Mountain Bluebird [*Sialia currucoides*]

During 1930–31, the Nevada Federation of Women's Clubs polled both schoolchildren and adult Nevada residents to learn which was the most popular bird in the state. It turned out to be the mountain bluebird. Many years later, on April 4, 1967, this bird was finally adopted as Nevada's state bird. The mountain bluebird is also *Idaho*'s state bird. It is described under that state.

NEW HAMPSHIRE

★ ━━━━━━━━━━━━━━━━━━━━ ★

Purple Finch [*Carpodacus purpureus*]

The purple finch is a small songbird about 6 inches (15 cm) long. As its name suggests, this bird has reddish-purple feathers with dark-brown shading on parts of its back, wings, and tail. The purple finch lives mostly on weeds and seeds. It has strong jaw muscles that allow it to eat hard seeds.

Several citizens' groups concerned with wildlife wanted the purple finch to be chosen as New Hampshire's state bird. The New Hampshire legislature debated over choosing the purple finch or the New Hampshire hen. The elected official who introduced the bill sponsoring the purple finch urged the legislature to act speedily "before some other state beats us to it." A majority of the legislators agreed, and the purple finch was officially adopted as New Hampshire's state bird on April 25, 1957.

NEW JERSEY

★ ━━━━━━━━ ★

Goldfinch [*Spinus tristis tristis*]

The goldfinch was adopted as New Jersey's state bird on July 27, 1935. The bird is found throughout the state. In the summer, groups of goldfinches are often seen sitting on fence posts or birdbaths.

The goldfinch is described under *Iowa*.

NEW MEXICO

★ ▬▬▬▬▬▬ ★

Roadrunner [*Geococcyx californianus*]

The roadrunner, also known as the chaparral cock, ground cuckoo, and snake killer, is a brown-feathered bird about 2 feet (61 cm) long. The bird's tail accounts for about half its length. In the sunlight, the roadrunner's feathers take on a greenish tint that helps it blend with its environment. This protection, or camouflage, makes it harder for the bird's enemies to see it. Roadrunners have strong legs and a feathered crest on top of their head.

Although roadrunners can fly, these birds spend most of their time on the ground. They can move quickly, sometimes traveling as fast as 15 miles (24 km) an hour. In the past, roadrunners delighted New Mexico pioneers, as the birds comically tried to keep pace with the wagon trains. On March 16, 1949, the roadrunner was officially made New Mexico's state bird.

▬▬▬▬▬

NEW YORK

Bluebird [*Sialia sialis*]

In New York State, a poll taken by the New York Federated Women's Club showed the bluebird to be a favorite among New Yorkers. It became their state bird on May 18, 1970.

The bluebird is described under *Missouri*.

NORTH CAROLINA

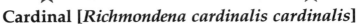

Cardinal [*Richmondena cardinalis cardinalis*]

North Carolina officially made the cardinal its state bird on March 4, 1943. The North Carolina Bird Club polled state residents to select a state bird, and the cardinal received the most votes. The birds live in the state throughout the year. In North Carolina, the cardinal is sometimes called the "winter redbird" because it is usually the only bird of that color seen during the colder months.

The cardinal is described under *Illinois*.

NORTH DAKOTA

★ ★

Western Meadowlark [*Sturnella neglecta*]

The people of North Dakota felt the western meadowlark best represented their state. Therefore, North Dakota's 30th Legislative Assembly officially adopted it as the state bird on March 10, 1947. North Dakota chose the western meadowlark even though five other states had already adopted the popular, pleasant-sounding bird.

The western meadowlark is described under *Kansas*.

OHIO

Cardinal [*Richmondena cardinalis cardinalis*]

In Ohio, the cardinal became the state bird on March 2, 1933. As in a number of other states, the cardinal lives year-round in Ohio. There residents have long enjoyed its dazzling color and musical sound.

The cardinal is described under *Illinois.*

OKLAHOMA

★ ━━━━━━━━━ ★

Scissor-Tailed Flycatcher [*Muscivora forficata*]

The scissor-tailed flycatcher is a long bird that may grow to a full 13 inches (33 cm). It has a light-colored head and red under its wing and lower belly. The bird gets the first part of its name from its long tail, which looks like a pair of scissor handles.

The scissor-tailed flycatcher eats grasshoppers, crickets, and other insects. It can even catch flying insects in midair. It quickly flies out from its perch to snatch its prey.

The scissor-tailed flycatcher was adopted as Oklahoma's state bird on May 26, 1951, replacing the bobwhite. The scissor-tailed flycatcher was thought to be more popular than the bobwhite among the state's residents. Its supporters had also argued that the scissor-tailed flycatcher is largely found in Oklahoma and the surrounding states while the bobwhite inhabits much of the country.

OREGON

Western Meadowlark [*Sturnella neglecta*]

In the spring of 1927, the Audubon Society held a contest in which Oregon schoolchildren were asked to pick their favorite bird. Although many birds were named, the western meadowlark was the most popular. It officially became Oregon's state bird on July 18, 1927.

The western meadowlark is described under *Kansas*.

PENNSYLVANIA

★ ▬▬▬▬▬▬▬▬▬▬▬▬▬▬▬ ★

Ruffed Grouse [*Bonasa umbellus*]

The ruffed grouse is a wild game bird. It is sometimes hunted and eaten in much the same way as wild duck or pheasant is. Although the ruffed grouse grows to about the size of a chicken, it tends to have a plumper body.

Pennsylvania's ruffed grouse has speckled reddish-brown feathers. Even the bird's legs are feather-covered for warmth.

The ruffed grouse was adopted as Pennsylvania's state bird on June 22, 1931.

▬▬▬▬▬▬▬▬▬

RHODE ISLAND

★ ▬▬▬▬▬▬▬▬▬ ★

Rhode Island Red Hen [*Gallus domesticus*]

The Rhode Island Red hen, a medium-sized chicken with red earlobes and yellow skin, became Rhode Island's state bird on May 3, 1954. It won a statewide contest in which Rhode Island residents of all ages voted. Other birds in the running included the towhee, osprey, hummingbird, and bobwhite. In previous years, the bobwhite had often been unofficially considered the state bird.

The Rhode Island Red hen was developed over 100 years ago in Rhode Island as a new breed of chicken. It all started when Rhode Island farmer William Tripp returned from a visit to Massachusetts with a large red rooster. The bird he brought back had been captured off southeast Asia's coast by a sailor. After the rooster bred with some of Tripp's hens, the farmer noticed that a superior chicken had been produced. His neighbors nicknamed these birds "Tripp fowls."

Nearby farmers, along with two professors from the state college, became involved in crossbreeding the chicken. The new breed was named the Rhode Island Red hen. Today these chickens are regarded as outstanding poultry throughout the world.

SOUTH CAROLINA

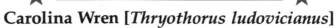

Carolina Wren [*Thryothorus ludovicianus*]

The Carolina wren is a brownish-red bird that measures about 5½ inches (14 cm) in length. It has a noticeable white stripe over its eyes and thin black bars on its tail. When the bird becomes excited, its tail points straight up. The Carolina wren is known for its pleasant song. It seems to repeatedly sing the word "teakettle teakettle teakettle."

This bird is found throughout South Carolina. It is at home in cities, on coastal beach areas, and on the state's highest mountains.

For many years, the Carolina wren was commonly considered the state bird. However, in 1939, the state's General Assembly passed a law naming the mockingbird as the state bird. But the wren's popularity among the people of South Carolina soon became clear. Legislators received many petitions urging that the law be changed in favor of the Carolina wren. Finally, in 1948, the law was repealed and a new law made the Carolina wren the official state bird on April 3, 1948.

SOUTH DAKOTA

Ring-Necked Pheasant [*Phasianus colchicus torquatus*]

The ring-necked pheasant is a midwestern game bird prized for its delicious meat. The magnificently colored male bird grows to 33 inches (84 cm) long including its tail. Its body is white, brown, and black, with shiny blue-green feathers covering its head and neck. Some males have a white ring around their neck. Females are smaller and less colorful. They may grow up to 21 inches (53 cm) long and have speckled brown bodies.

The ring-necked pheasant was first found in China. The ancient Romans later spread the bird throughout Europe. It was brought to South Dakota in 1898 and adopted as the state bird on February 13, 1943.

TENNESSEE

★ ▬▬▬▬▬▬▬▬ ★

Mockingbird [*Mimus polyglottos*]

According to the Nashville *Banner*, a Tennessee newspaper, the Tennessee Ornithological Society (a group concerned with birds) held a poll to pick a state bird. The mockingbird received the most votes and officially became Tennessee's state bird on April 22, 1933.

The mockingbird is described under *Arkansas*.

TEXAS

Mockingbird [*Mimus polyglottos*]

The Texas Federation of Women's Clubs suggested that the mockingbird be made the state bird. It was adopted by the state legislature on January 31, 1927. It was chosen for its song and because it defends its home (nest) "like any true Texan."

The mockingbird is described under *Arkansas*.

UTAH

★ ▬▬ ★

Sea Gull [*Larus californicus*]

The sea gull is a long-winged bird about the size of a crow or larger. The adult sea gull's body is usually gray on top and white underneath. These birds live near large bodies of water. They eat small water animals, insects, worms, and bits of garbage found floating on the water.

During the early pioneer days, gulls were extremely helpful to Utah settlers. In the spring of 1848, hoards of hungry crickets greedily attacked the settlers' newly planted grain. The settlers tried to stop the pests by digging water-filled trenches around their farms and even setting fires. But the crickets continued to devour their crops. The pioneers prayed for a miracle that would save them from starvation.

The answer to their prayers came in the form of a large flock of gulls, which flew in from the Great Salt Lake. The gulls quickly ate the crickets, saving the small portion of grain that the insects had not yet destroyed.

Grateful to the gulls, Utah later passed a law forbidding their destruction. In 1955 the sea gull was made the state's official bird. A monument has also been built to honor these birds.

▬▬▬

VERMONT

★ ━━━━━━ ★

Hermit Thrush [*Catharus guttatus*]

The hermit thrush is a brown songbird with a whitish speckled breast. The bird inhabits woodland areas and spends much of its time on the ground and in the low branches of trees and shrubs.

Some Vermont legislators were against adopting the hermit thrush as the state bird. They argued that the hermit thrush is not a genuine Vermont bird because it migrates south during the cold winter months. Those legislators suggested that either the crow or bluejay represent the state since both these birds remain in Vermont year-round.

However, the hermit thrush eventually won out in the state legislature and was officially adopted on June 1, 1941. This was partly because the bird could be found in all of Vermont's fourteen counties. It was also thought that state residents had long been enchanted by its beautiful flutelike song.

━━━━━━

VIRGINIA

Cardinal [*Richmondena cardinalis cardinalis*]

Virginia adopted the cardinal as its state bird on January 15, 1950. Virginians chose the cardinal for its bright-red feathers and "cheerful song." In the state the cardinal is often called the "Virginia redbird."

The cardinal is described under *Illinois.*

WASHINGTON

★ ━━━━━━━━━━ ★

Willow Goldfinch [*Spinus tristis*]

In Washington, selecting a state bird took quite a bit of time. The western meadowlark was the choice of Washington schoolchildren in 1928. However, when the legislators learned that a number of other states had already chosen the meadowlark, they didn't act on the children's suggestion. Then in 1931 the Washington Federation of Women's Clubs held a statewide poll to determine Washington's most popular bird. The goldfinch won by a large number of votes.

Although Washington now had two choices for state bird, neither had been officially adopted. In fact, no action was taken until twenty-two years later, when the state's schoolchildren were again asked to cast their ballots for state bird. This time they picked the goldfinch. On March 19, 1951, the willow goldfinch officially became Washington's state bird.

The goldfinch is described under *Iowa*.

━━━━━━━

WEST VIRGINIA

★ ━━━━━━━━━━━━ ★

Cardinal [*Richmondena cardinalis cardinalis*]

In West Virginia, a statewide poll was conducted to determine the residents' favorite bird. The cardinal won the contest. The robin received the second-largest number of votes, while the redheaded woodpecker came in last. On March 7, 1949, the cardinal officially became West Virginia's state bird.

The cardinal is described under *Illinois*.

Female Cardinal

WISCONSIN

Robin [*Turdus migratorius*]

In Wisconsin during the school year of 1926–27, schoolchildren were asked to choose a state bird. When the ballots were counted, the robin received twice as many votes as any other bird. On June 9, 1949, nearly twenty-two years later, the Wisconsin legislature finally adopted it as the state bird.

The robin is described under *Connecticut*.

WYOMING

★ ━━━━━━ ★

Western Meadowlark [*Sturnella neglecta*]

There's an old Wyoming story about how Mother Nature helped choose Wyoming's state bird long before humans ever thought of having state birds. According to the tale, Mother Nature asked all the birds to choose either the bluebird for happiness, the robin for its cheery call, or the meadowlark for its beautiful song. They picked the meadowlark.

On February 5, 1927, Wyoming legislators followed the tale's example when they chose the meadowlark as the state's official bird. Although the bill passed by Wyoming's legislature did not mention a particular type of meadowlark, only the western meadowlark is found in that region.

The western meadowlark is described under *Kansas*.

━━━━━━

FOR FURTHER READING

Burnie, David. *Birds*. New York: Knopf, 1988.

Cole, Joanna. *A Bird's Body*. New York: Morrow, 1982.

Esbensen, Barbara Juster. *Great Northern Diver: The Loon*. Boston: Little, Brown, 1990.

Gans, Roma. *When Birds Change Their Feathers*. New York: Crowell, 1980.

Hirschi, Ron. *The Mountain Bluebird*. New York: Cobblehill, 1990.

McGowen, Tom. *Album of Birds*. New York: Macmillan, 1982.

Selsam, Millicent E., and Joyce Hunt. *A First Look at Bird's Nests*. New York: Walker, 1984.

Stone, Lynn. *Birds of Prey*. Chicago: Childrens Press, 1983.

INDEX

★ ━━━ ★

Alabama, 9
Alaska, 10
Arizona, 11
Arkansas, 12

Baltimore oriole (Maryland
state bird), 30
Bluebird (Missouri, New York
state bird), 35, 42
Blue Hen chicken (Delaware
state bird), 17
Brown pelican (Louisiana
state bird), 28
Brown thrasher (Georgia state
bird), 20

Cactus wren (Arizona state
bird), 11
California, 13
California valley quail
(California state bird), 13
Cardinal (Illinois, Indiana,
Kentucky, North Carolina,
Ohio, Virginia, West
Virginia state bird), 23, 24,
27, 43, 45, 56, 58
Carolina wren (South
Carolina state bird), 50
Chickadee (Maine,
Massachusetts state bird),
29, 31
Colorado, 14

Connecticut, 16

Delaware, 17
District of Columbia, 18

Eastern goldfinch (Iowa state
bird), 25

Florida, 19

Georgia, 20
Goldfinch (New Jersey state
bird), 40

Hawaii, 21
Hermit thrush (Vermont state
bird), 55

Idaho, 22
Illinois, 23
Indiana, 24
Iowa, 25

Kansas, 26
Kentucky, 27

Lark bunting (Colorado state
bird), 14
Loon (Minnesota state bird),
33
Louisiana, 28

Maine, 29

Maryland, 30
Massachusetts, 31
Michigan, 32
Minnesota, 33
Mississippi, 34
Missouri, 35
Mockingbird (Arkansas,
   Florida, Mississippi,
   Tennessee, Texas state
   bird), 12, 19, 34, 52, 53
Montana, 36
Mountain bluebird (Idaho,
   Nevada state bird), 22, 38

Nebraska, 37
Nene (Hawaii state bird), 21
Nevada, 38
New Hampshire, 39
New Jersey, 40
New Mexico, 41
New York, 42
North Carolina, 43
North Dakota, 44

Ohio, 45
Oklahoma, 46
Oregon, 47

Pennsylvania, 48
Puerto Rico, 15
Purple finch (New Hampshire
   state bird), 39

Reinita común (Puerto Rico),
   15
Rhode Island, 49
Rhode Island Red hen (Rhode
   Island state bird), 49
Ring-necked pheasant (South
   Dakota state bird), 51

Roadrunner (New Mexico
   state bird), 41
Robin (Connecticut,
   Michigan, Wisconsin state
   bird), 16, 32, 59
Ruffed grouse (Pennsylvania
   state bird), 48

Scissor-tailed flycatcher
   (Oklahoma state bird), 46
Sea gull (Utah state bird), 54
South Carolina, 50
South Dakota, 51

Tennessee, 52
Texas, 53

Utah, 54

Vermont, 55
Virginia, 56

Washington, 57
Western meadowlark
   (Kansas, Montana,
   Nebraska, North Dakota,
   Oregon, Wyoming state
   bird), 26, 36, 37, 44, 47, 60
West Virginia, 58
Willow goldfinch
   (Washington state bird), 57
Willow ptarmigan (Alaska
   state bird), 10
Wisconsin, 59
Wood thrush (District of
   Columbia state bird), 18
Wyoming, 60

Yellowhammer (Alabama
   state bird), 9

ABOUT THE AUTHOR

Elaine Landau has written more than forty-five books and articles for young people. She loves her work, taking walks in the country with her dog, Maxi, and watching the brightly colored goldfinches perch on the trees and fence surrounding her New Jersey home. Cardinals and bluejays are also frequent visitors to her backyard.